POWERED BY STEAM

Kristy Stark, M.A.Ed.

✳ Smithsonian

© 2019 Smithsonian Institution. The name "Smithsonian" and the Smithsonian logo are registered trademarks owned by the Smithsonian Institution.

Contributing Author

Heather Schultz, M.A.

Consultants

Timothy Winkle
Museum Curator, Division of Home and Community Life
National Museum of American History

Tamieka Grizzle, Ed.D.
K–5 STEM Lab Instructor
Harmony Leland Elementary School

Stephanie Anastasopoulos, M.Ed.
TOSA, STREAM Integration
Solana Beach School District

Publishing Credits

Rachelle Cracchiolo, M.S.Ed., *Publisher*
Conni Medina, M.A.Ed., *Managing Editor*
Diana Kenney, M.A.Ed., NBCT, *Series Developer*
Véronique Bos, *Creative Director*
June Kikuchi, *Content Director*
Robin Erickson, *Art Director*
Seth Rogers, *Editor*
Mindy Duits, *Senior Graphic Designer*
Smithsonian Science Education Center

Image Credits: p.6 Sheila Terry/Science Source; p.7 (top), p.9 (left), p.10, p.13 Science Source; p.8, p.11 Look and Learn/Bridgeman Images; p.9 (right) SPL/Science Source; p.12 (middle) Library of Congress [LC-DIG-nclc-02873]; p.14 Waterhouse & Dodd, London, UK/Bridgeman Images; p.15 (top), p.16 (right) Public Domain via Wikimedia; p.15 (bottom) British Library/Science Source; p.16 (left), p.18 New York Public Library/Science Source; p.17 Goddard Automotive/Alamy; p.20 Clarence O. Becker Archive/Alamy; p.21 SPL RM Images / Science Source; p.23 Ed Young/Science Source; pp.26–27 Hindustan Times/Sipa USA/Newscom; all other images from iStock and/or Shutterstock.

Library of Congress Cataloging-in-Publication Data

Names: Stark, Kristy, author.
Title: Powered by steam / Kristy Stark.
Description: Huntington Beach, CA : Teacher Created Materials, Inc., [2019] | Includes index. | Audience: Grades 4 to 6. |
Identifiers: LCCN 2018005253 (print) | LCCN 2018013533 (ebook) | ISBN 9781493869343 (E-book) | ISBN 9781493866946 (pbk.)
Subjects: LCSH: Steam-engines--Juvenile literature. | Steam--Juvenile literature.
Classification: LCC TJ467 (ebook) | LCC TJ467 .S73 2019 (print) | DDC 621.1--dc23
LC record available at https://lccn.loc.gov/2018005253

◉ Smithsonian

© 2019 Smithsonian Institution. The name "Smithsonian" and the Smithsonian logo are registered trademarks owned by the Smithsonian Institution.

Teacher Created Materials

5301 Oceanus Drive
Huntington Beach, CA 92649-1030
www.tcmpub.com
ISBN 978-1-4938-6694-6
©2019 Teacher Created Materials, Inc.

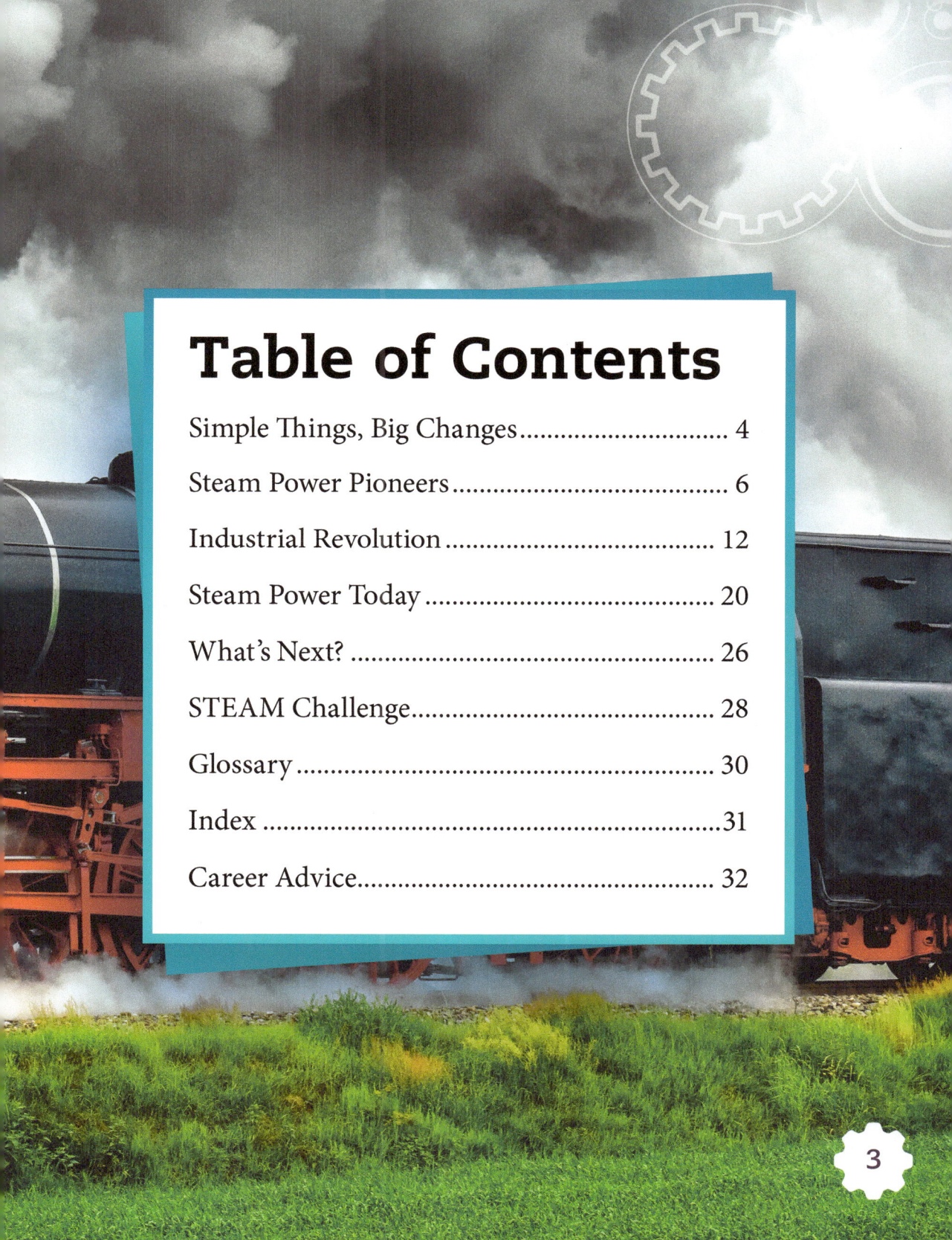

Table of Contents

Simple Things, Big Changes 4

Steam Power Pioneers 6

Industrial Revolution 12

Steam Power Today 20

What's Next? 26

STEAM Challenge 28

Glossary 30

Index 31

Career Advice 32

Simple Things, Big Changes

People use devices and tools that make life easier. Computers and smartphones have changed the way people live. Technology has made our lives easier in many ways. But technology needs power.

Early technology was powered by people. Later, animals were used. But, the amount of power they produced was limited. In the late 1600s, scientists and engineers found that steam could be used to power new technology.

A family uses technology to talk to each other.

Doctors use technology like this tablet to help them do their job.

Steam is the gaseous form of water. It is made when water boils. This happens at 100° Celsius (212° Fahrenheit) at sea level. A lot of energy is produced when water turns to steam. People found that this energy could be stored and used to power machines and devices.

steam

Water is made when two hydrogen **atoms** and one oxygen atom combine. That is why it is referred to as H_2O!

Steam Power Pioneers

Steam power has been used for a long time. In fact, it was used in the first century. Heron of Alexandria made a device that used steam to turn a sphere. But his device did not do much more than that. It served as a toy to amuse his friends.

There was a lot of progress in steam engineering in the seventeenth century. Many people were drawn to science. They developed new **theories** and tested their ideas.

Heron shows how his device works.

Denis Papin

Denis Papin (deh-NEE pa-PEEN) was a French inventor. He studied the **properties** of steam and air. He was one of the first people to know that air contained **matter**. Papin also proved that a space could have no matter in it. That space is called a vacuum. He believed that if air had matter, it could create pressure, especially within a vacuum. He experimented with steam, air, and vacuums. He wanted to use these ideas to build a machine.

Denis Papin

The Air We Breathe

When we breathe, our lungs fill with air. Air is made up of matter. Matter is anything that takes up space and has weight. We can't see air, but it uses space and has weight. You can see this when you blow air into a balloon!

Papin's machine used steam to create a vacuum. It started by heating water to make steam. The steam was stored under pressure. This pressure created enough energy to move the parts of the machine.

Papin thought that steam would one day be used to power ships and factories. He dreamed of building a larger machine that would power them. Although he never built this bigger device, he paved the way for others.

Papin works in a lab.

Thomas Savery

Thomas Savery was an English engineer. He worked to build a steam-powered pump. The pump would remove water from coal mines. Water in mines was a big problem. It kept workers from being able to access coal.

The pump heated water in a boiler. Then, the steam was sprayed with cold water in another container. This made the steam **condense**. As the steam condensed, it made a vacuum. The vacuum pushed the water up and out of the mine to reveal precious coal and minerals.

Savery's machine

Savery called his machine the "Miner's Friend."

Thomas Newcomen

Thomas Newcomen (NOO-kuh-muhn) lived in England. He sold mining equipment. He did not want to see mines shut down because of water. Fewer open mines would mean less business for him. It would mean less work for miners, too.

Newcomen worked with a mechanic named John Calley. They improved upon the ideas of Savery and Papin.

They spent 10 years working on a steam engine. It was similar to Papin's. It used steam and cold water. It condensed steam to make a vacuum. Papin's machine was powered by pressure from steam. Newcomen's machine used pressure from steam, too. But it also used pressure from the air around the working parts. The combination of pressures gave the machine more power.

In 1712, the pump was put in a mineshaft. It removed water from the deep mine. It was a huge success! Newcomen got hundreds of orders for his pump.

Newcomen's machine

A worker adds coal to heat the water in Newcomen's machine.

Newcomen's machine could pump thousands of gallons of water per hour.

Industrial Revolution

In the past, people made things in their homes and in small workshops. They made their own cloth and clothes. They grew their own food. They used whatever tools or simple machines they had. Then, the Industrial Revolution began in Britain in the late 1700s.

Goods could now be made more quickly by machines. Factories could **mass-produce** goods. Most of the machines used were powered by coal. Thanks to Newcomen's steam engine, miners brought in huge amounts of coal.

A child works long hours in a factory during the Industrial Revolution.

coal

James Watt

In Scotland, James Watt made tools at a university. One day in 1764, a steam engine was brought in to be fixed. It was a Newcomen steam pump! While he tried to fix it, Watt found ways to improve the machine. He found how to make it more **efficient**.

Watt redesigned the engine to cut back on the loss of steam. He found that the cold water that condensed the steam was cooling the **cylinder**, too. This was a problem.

James Watt

TECHNOLOGY

Making Engines Today

Machines help car factories make hundreds of engines each day. First, machines are used to melt steel and aluminum. These melted metals are then poured into molds. Other machines use heated metals to make an engine's smaller parts. Then, machines trim and polish the parts. After that, engine parts are put together.

Cooling the cylinder caused the machine to lose steam. Less steam meant less power. Watt thought the loss of steam could be stopped if the cylinder stayed as hot as the steam. This idea led him to invent a separate condenser. The condenser was a second chamber where steam could cool and condense. This kept the cylinder hot. Watt put another layer of metal around the cylinder to help it remain hot. He called it a steam jacket.

In 1769, Watt got a patent for his new design. Over the next 30 years, Watt and his company made more than five hundred steam engines.

Watt continued to build steam engines. He also built a rotary steam engine. This engine powered things that needed to spin. Many factories used this type of steam engine.

Watt's designs shaped the future of technology. In fact, Watt is known as the master of the steam engine.

Watt plays with steam from a teapot as a child.

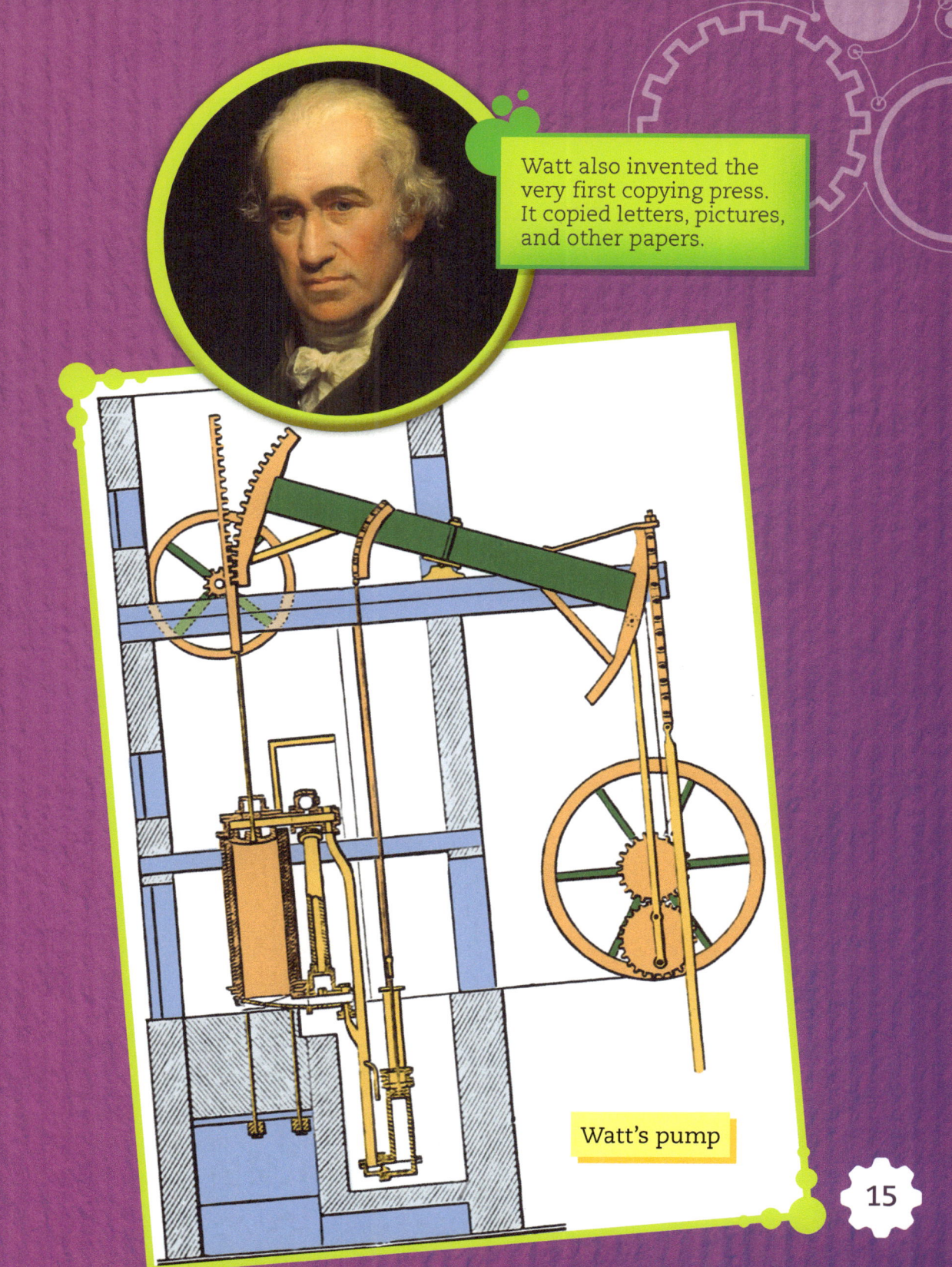

Watt also invented the very first copying press. It copied letters, pictures, and other papers.

Watt's pump

Richard Trevithick

Richard Trevithick (TREH-vih-thik) was a scientist who used Watt's ideas. He built an engine that used high-pressure steam. The steam expanded in the cylinder. It created a large amount of power. To avoid explosions, he used a boiler with thick walls. The walls needed to hold up to the high pressure.

Trevithick found that his engine did not need a vacuum. He linked the **piston** rod directly to the wheel or pump. The engine did not need to condense steam. So steam was allowed to seep out.

The engine had great power. It ran a carriage and could be used to drive people around London. In 1801, it moved its first passengers. Two years later, Trevithick built a new steam engine.

In 1804, Trevithick built the first steam locomotive that ran on rails. It linked an iron mill to a canal for shipping. Before this, iron or coal from a mill was moved in carts by people or horses. Trevithick's engines paved the way for travel by steam locomotives.

Trevithick's engine

Richard Trevithick

This re-creation shows what Trevithick's steam carriage looked like.

ENGINEERING

Engineering Design Process

Engineers, such as Trevithick and Watt, work to solve problems. They often build upon the work of other people. They figure out what works and what doesn't work. They carefully consider how to improve ideas. Engineers use five basic steps as they design:

1. define the problem
2. research and brainstorm
3. design and build
4. test and improve
5. reflect and share

Robert Fulton

Soon, people began to think about using steam engines to run boats. An American named Robert Fulton worked to make this happen. Fulton was not the first to build a steamboat. He built upon the work of John Fitch, who made a small steamboat that powered a dozen paddles.

Fulton designed a steamboat that used Watt's engine. Fulton believed the engine could do more than run mills and pumps. He thought that steam-powered boats could move goods on rivers.

In 1807, his vision became reality. Fulton's steamboat was named *Clermont*. It carried goods on the Hudson River from New York City to Albany. The boat went about 8 kilometers (5 miles) per hour upstream. It was much faster than using a vehicle to haul goods over hilly areas. Soon, Fulton had boats on six major rivers in the United States. Steamboats played a key role in trade around the world. They helped people explore and expand the United States, too.

drawing of Fulton's steam engine

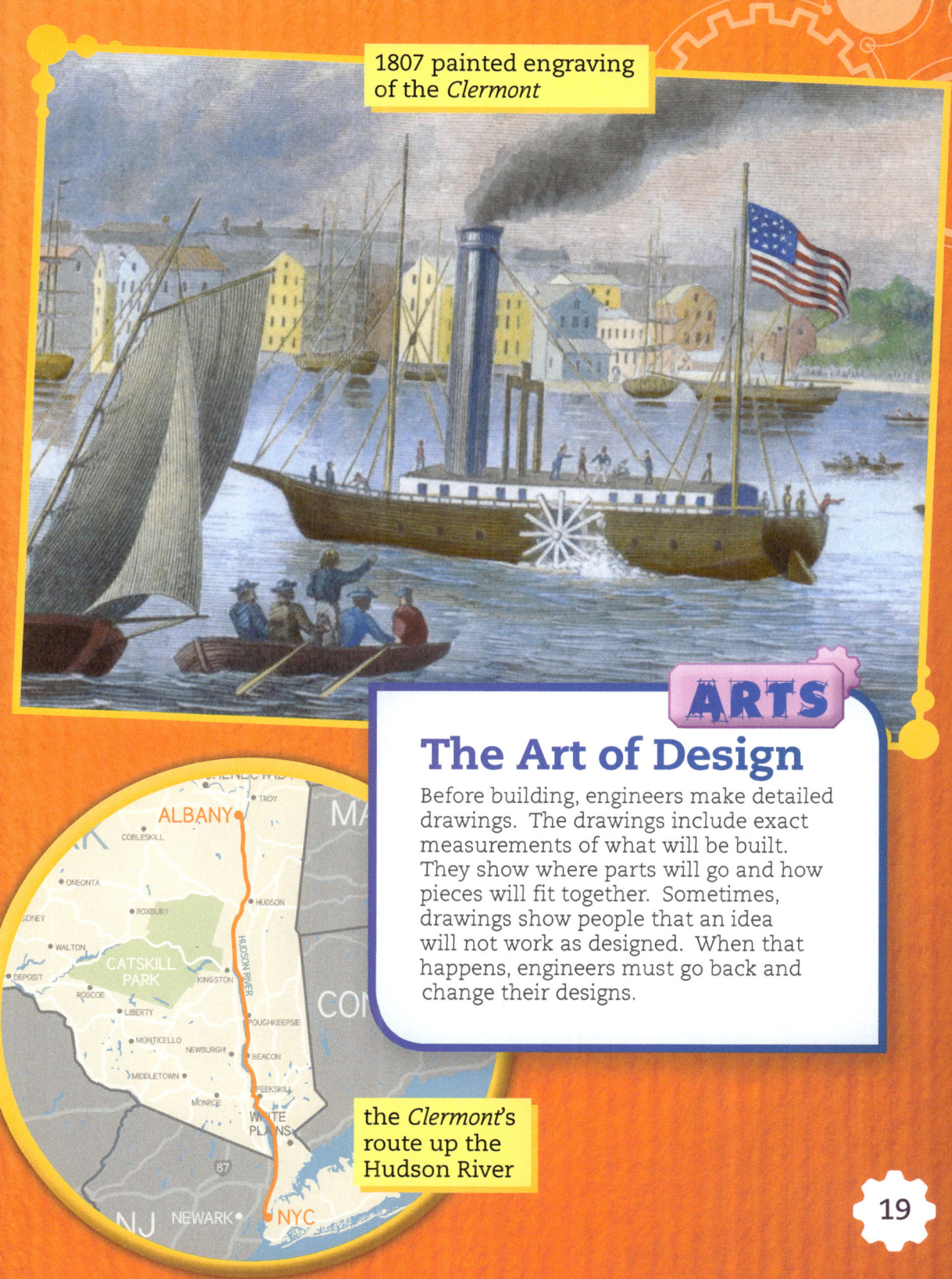

1807 painted engraving of the *Clermont*

the *Clermont*'s route up the Hudson River

ARTS

The Art of Design

Before building, engineers make detailed drawings. The drawings include exact measurements of what will be built. They show where parts will go and how pieces will fit together. Sometimes, drawings show people that an idea will not work as designed. When that happens, engineers must go back and change their designs.

Steam Power Today

Steam power was once the main source of power for engines. It was fueled by coal. But air became polluted from burning too much coal. Soon, the amount of available coal began to shrink. Inventors and engineers found ways to use gasoline to run engines. They found ways to use methods such as nuclear power to create electricity, too. Many of these resources are cleaner options than coal. Now, steam power is used mainly to make electricity.

Coal is still used to make about one-third of the electricity in the United States.

A train runs on steam created by burning coal.

Generating Electricity

Steam affects most people's daily lives. Steam is used to run generators, which can bring electricity to homes, schools, and businesses. Steam is used in a similar way as it was to run mills and pumps. First, water is heated by gas or some other source, such as solar power. Next, water is converted into steam in a boiler. Then, steam is pumped into a steam turbine.

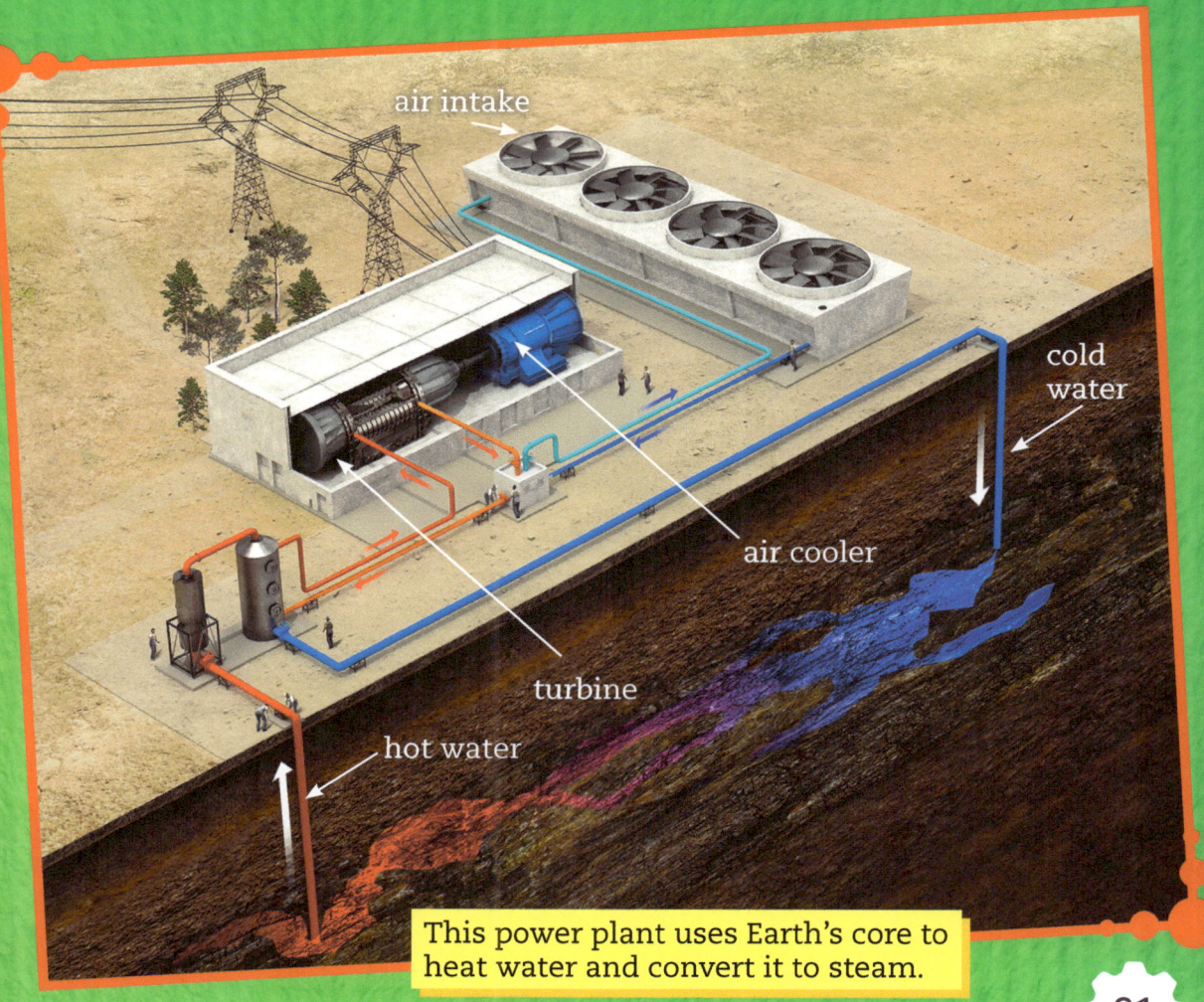

This power plant uses Earth's core to heat water and convert it to steam.

The movement of steam spins the blades of the turbine. The turbine makes the generator spin. Energy from the generator pushes electric charges. This makes usable power.

The used steam is then cooled. It is released into the air. It does not pollute the air because it is just water in the form of a gas. Steam will likely be used to make electricity for many years to come.

Recovering Heat Loss

Steam is not only used to make electricity on land. It is used to generate power on large ships, too. Most cruise ships use gas turbines. These turbines provide most of the power for the ships. But gas turbines lose a lot of heat as they work. So ships also have steam turbines. Steam turbines use heat that comes from a gas turbine's **exhaust**.

This process converts more energy to electricity. It is used to heat water and run air-conditioning on ships. Power generated from steam turbines helps passengers feel more comfortable on the ships!

exhaust from a cruise ship

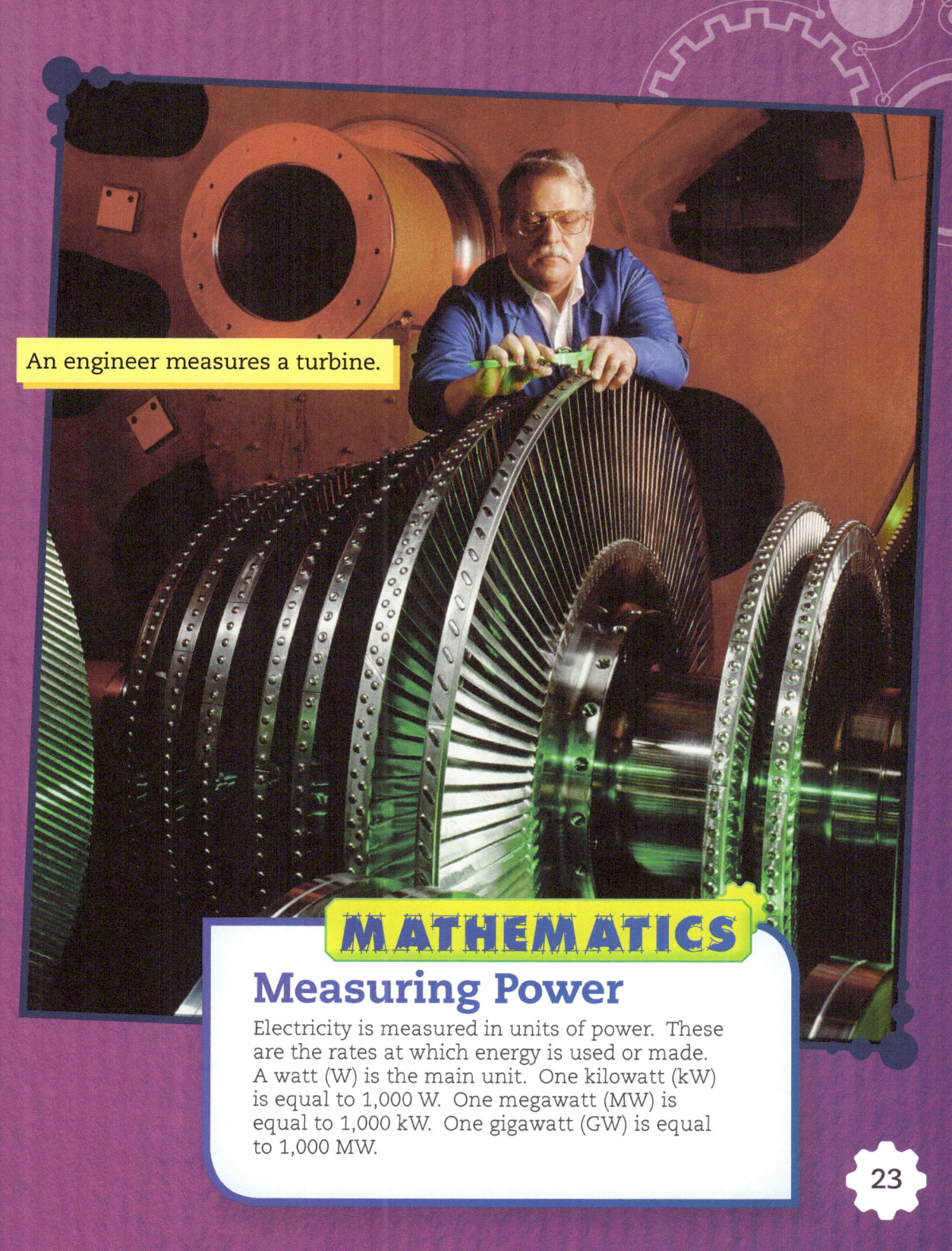

An engineer measures a turbine.

MATHEMATICS
Measuring Power

Electricity is measured in units of power. These are the rates at which energy is used or made. A watt (W) is the main unit. One kilowatt (kW) is equal to 1,000 W. One megawatt (MW) is equal to 1,000 kW. One gigawatt (GW) is equal to 1,000 MW.

Future Uses

Ships are not the only vessels that lose heat. Cars lose heat through exhaust, too. Engineers are testing ways to recover this heat loss. They hope to use it to run cars one day.

Engineers are also working to build a gas engine that will collect steam. The engine will make high-pressure steam. As Trevithick found years ago, high-pressure steam has a lot of power. Engineers plan to route steam back into the main engine. Then, steam will power the pistons. So, the engine would be a **hybrid** of steam and gas power!

Experts hope to use this concept on food delivery trucks, too. These trucks have refrigeration units. The units keep food cold until it is delivered to stores. The hybrid steam engine may be able to help cool the trucks by using the exhaust heat.

refrigerated delivery truck

POWER CONTROL UNIT
ENGINE
Electricity
GENERATOR
MOTOR

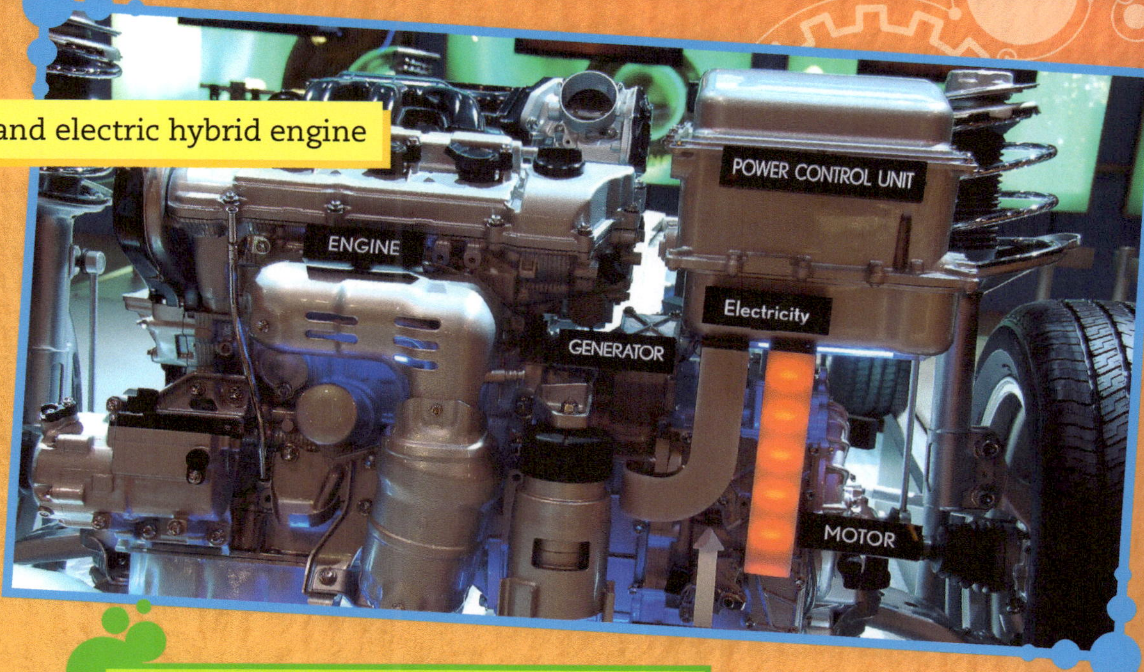

gas and electric hybrid engine

Engineers estimate that about one-third of energy is lost in a car's exhaust heat.

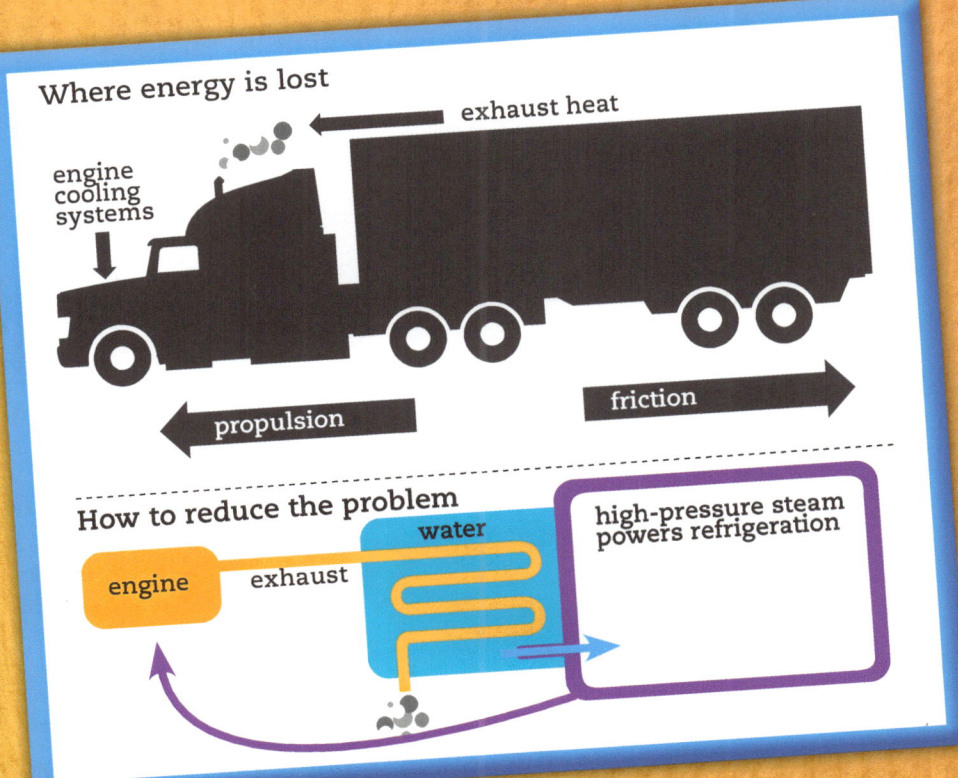

Where energy is lost
exhaust heat
engine cooling systems
propulsion
friction
How to reduce the problem
water
high-pressure steam powers refrigeration
engine
exhaust

What's Next?

Something as simple as steam has had a huge impact on engineering advances. But there are other ways to power machines. Engineers have found ways to harness the energy of the sun. It powers electricity in homes and offices. Engineers have found ways to use water to provide power, too. The strong force of rushing water is used to power turbines in the same way that steam is used. The force of wind is used to generate electricity, too.

Steam, sun, water, and wind are all around us. They are all simple things, but they have changed how electricity is made and used. That is not an easy task!

So, what simple things might be used in the future? It is hard to predict. But engineers continue to have new ideas. They try new things. Perhaps you might solve a big problem some day. The possibilities are endless!

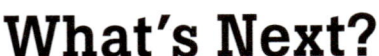
An engineer works at a power plant.

This diagram shows how ocean tides are used to make energy.

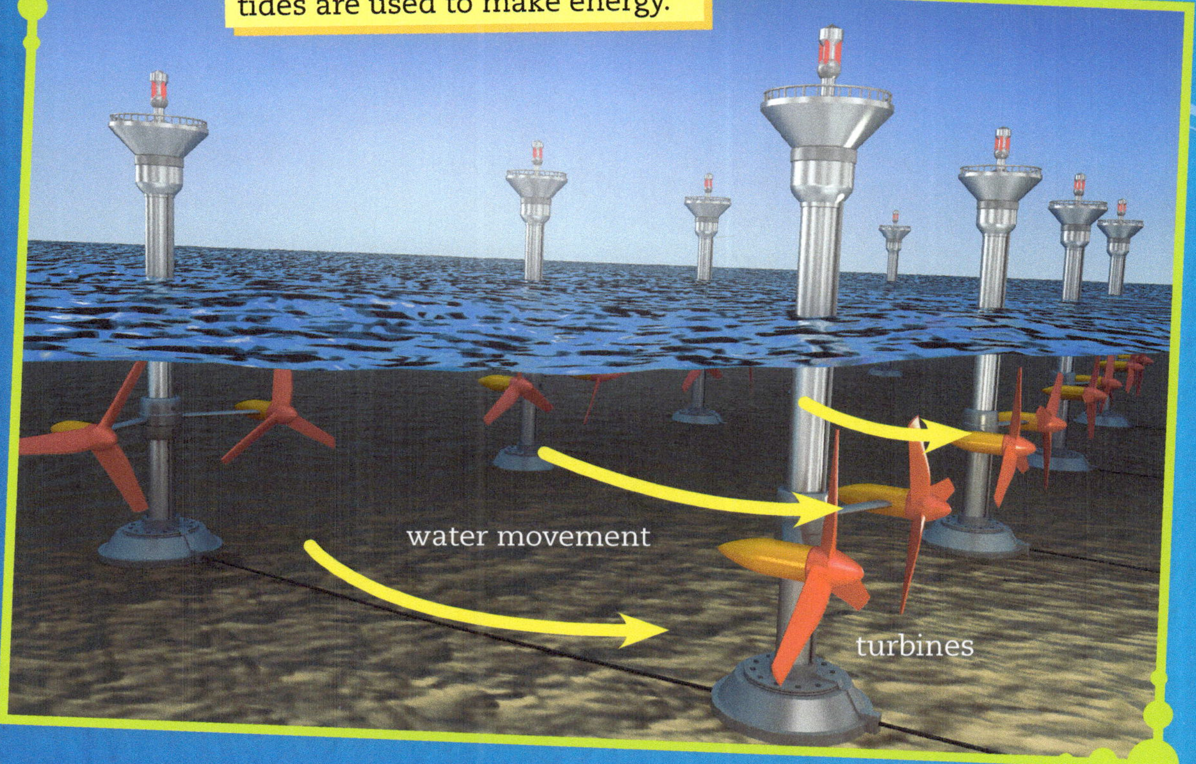

water movement

turbines

The largest solar plant in the world is in southern India. It creates enough energy to power about 150,000 homes.

27

STEAM CHALLENGE

Define the Problem

Heat loss can be a problem when powering a steam engine. It can also be a problem in everyday life. Your task is to alter a container's design to keep water hot longer than a regular container.

 **Constraints:** You may not use more than five materials to alter your container. The container must hold a ½ liter (about 2 cups) of liquid.

 **Criteria:** Your altered container must keep a ½ L (about 2 c.) of hot water at a higher temperature than a ½ L (about 2 c.) of hot water in a similar but unaltered container after 10 minutes.

Research and Brainstorm

How can you limit the amount of heat water loses over time? What kinds of materials can stop heat from escaping?

Design and Build

Sketch your design. What materials will work best? Why did you choose these materials? Alter the container.

Test and Improve

Pour ½ L (about 2 c.) of hot water into your altered container and the same amount into a similar but unaltered container. Measure the temperature every 2 minutes for 10 minutes. Did it work? Modify your design and try again.

Reflect and Share

How would the challenge change if you wanted to keep water cold rather than hot? Would your design change? Why or why not?

Glossary

atoms—tiny particles that make up everything that takes up space

condense—to change from a less dense form to a denser form, such as from a gas to a liquid

cylinder—a tube in which a piston of an engine moves

efficient—capable of producing the desired results without wasting materials, time, or energy

exhaust—a mixture of gases produced by an engine

gaseous—having the form of gas

generators—machines that produce electricity

hybrid—something that is formed by combining two or more things

mass-produce—to produce very large amounts of something by using machinery

matter—something that forms physical objects and occupies space

patent—an official document that gives a person or company the right to be the only one that makes or sells a product for a certain period of time

piston—a part of an engine that moves up and down inside a cylinder

properties—special characteristics of something

rotary—having a part that turns around a central point, such as a wheel

theories—rules that explain scientific phenomena

turbine—an engine with blades that spin by pressure from water, steam, or air

Index

Albany, New York, 18

Britain, 12

Calley, John, 10

Clermont, 18–19

engineering design process, 17

England, 10

Fitch, John, 18

Fulton, Robert, 18

Heron of Alexandria, 6

Hudson River, 18–19

London, 16

Miner's Friend, 9

Newcomen, Thomas, 10–13

New York City, 18

Papin, Denis, 7–8, 10

Savery, Thomas, 9–10

Scotland, 13

Trevithick, Richard, 16–17, 24

Watt, James, 13–18

CAREER ADVICE
from Smithsonian

Do you want to tell people about energy?
Here are some tips to get you started.

"I work at the National Postal Museum. One of the things I research and write about is the history of railway mail service. It was the fastest way to get mail from the east to the west coast of the United States in the mid-1800s. I get to study the science of steam power. I also study the history of objects powered by steam. Knowledge of history is important to do my job." —*Nancy Pope, Historian and Curator*

"To work at a museum, history and science are important. It is also important to love being curious. Find new objects. Figure out how to exhibit them to tell their story to the public." —*Megan Smith, Interpretive* Specialist